LODGE

LODGE

AN INDOORSY TOUR OF
AMERICA'S NATIONAL PARKS

MAX HUMPHREY

WITH KATHRYN O'SHEA-EVANS

PHOTOGRAPHS BY DAVID TSAY AND ROB SCHANZ

FOREWORD BY KEN BURNS

Gibbs Smith
TO ENRICH & INSPIRE HUMANKIND

FOREWORD

by Ken Burns

The architects tasked with designing the first National Park lodges had a problem. What structural style could accommodate road-weary travelers without marring the exultant beauty of the park itself? Slapdash tents wouldn't do in these lands of wild weather and wilder residents, like the free-range grizzlies and mountain lions who then roamed largely unfettered across the landscape in Yellowstone and Yosemite. Plus, even in the early twentieth century, park rangers were expecting a crowd. America would come to see this.

The answer came in what National Park staffers refer to as Parkitecture: a look that summons the cozy aesthetic of the alpine chalet with elements of each region's local grandeur, like native boulders and timber. If the National Parks were America's Best Idea, the lodges made it an idea worth exploring to the sometimes backcountry-averse travelers who occasionally arrived on a park's buggy doorstep. After a day afield, little says "Welcome, put up your boots and stay awhile" as much as riverstone fireplaces and soaring ceilings.

In *Lodge* you'll find ten of America's most beloved National Park lodges captured in all their allure for the next generation. There's Glacier's Lake McDonald Lodge, which edges a 472-foot-deep glacial lake and has Blackfoot words and phrases etched into the lobby's concrete floors. And Paradise Inn, with its parchment paper lanterns hand-painted with the plants that grow on adjacent Mt. Rainier.

Of course, most people don't travel all the way to the National Parks solely to stay at the lodges. And yet walking into one of these often century-old lobbies after years away—or even for the first time—can feel like coming home. Opening this book can be a bit like that, even if you're thumbing through it on a coffee table. Just add a whiff of woodsmoke and imagine that your next adventure is just around the bend.

INTRODUCTION

by Max Humphrey

I could gut a trout before I learned to read. I grew up in New England. I was outdoorsy. Days were spent in the woods behind my house building tree forts with the neighborhood kids until someone's mom yelled that it was dinnertime. We swam in ponds. We got bug bites. We popped wheelies. That all changed in the winter of 1986 when my parents surprised my brother and me with a Nintendo. I remember setting it up at my grandparents' apartment above their general store in Craftsbury, Vermont, and thinking "I'm never going outside again."

That feeling faded before the snow melted, but things were different. For every day I spent outside, I'd spend another inside. One day would be playing catch with my brother, the next would be playing Super Mario Brothers. I needed both. And I'm not alone. I'm sure a lot of you are indoorsy-outdoorsy too. We look forward to the after-hike fireside chats as much as the hikes themselves.

In my day job as an interior designer, I'm fueled by nostalgia. The homes I design for clients are all buffalo plaid and beadboard, just like my house growing up. But I take inspiration from all sorts of things. Travel and the National Parks always top the list. The historic lodges know exactly what they are—and they don't hold back. My obsession led me to want to photograph and write about our beloved National Parks, but from the inside.

Kid Max Humphrey
being outdoorsy.

When I would tell friends or family I was working on this book, they'd almost instantly offer up their own lodge memories: the best pancakes in the world they had as a kid at The Ahwahnee, or the college summer they spent scooping ice cream at Lake McDonald. Everyone has a connection; everybody has a story.

This book isn't going to delve into any secret hiking trails: it's an indoorsy guide. What it will do is give you a prime panorama of what to expect from a designer's perspective. Hopefully the photos will make you want to visit the parks, and the stories and descriptions will help you bring some of their iconic looks into your own home. There are a lot of design takeaways from the lodges: use local materials, arrange your living room seating in a way that encourages conversation, define your spaces with area rugs, and—when in doubt—paint everything forest green.

THE AHWAHNEE

Yosemite National Park, California

When I was working on this book, everybody grilled me on which lodge was my favorite—an impossible ask. Each one had something that set it apart from the rest of the pack. Lake Quinault was easily the most fun; Crater Lake the most inspiring (those stars!); the Oasis at Death Valley a total and luxurious surprise. But if you could only ever visit one lodge in your life, it has to be The Ahwahnee. It's the full package.

The journey to get here is part of the draw. To reach the legendary hotel, which sits tucked near the Merced River in Yosemite Valley, you drive through a series of actual Ansel Adams photographs: winding through the Sierra Nevada mountains, pulling over often to ogle 130-million-year-old Half Dome and Yosemite Falls. (Even though you can't wait to get to the lodge, you can't not stop.) We were there during an annual phenomenon called "firefall," when the setting sunlight hits 1,575-foot-tall Horsetail Fall in such a way that it makes the water glow like a bonfire as it bounds over the eastern granite face of El Capitan. And then we finally saw it—The Ahwahnee.

Opened in 1927, the Y-shaped lodge composed of rough-cut granite and concrete was meant to echo the cliffs surrounding it, and it does. Then-director of the National Park Service Stephen T. Mather was a bit peer-pressured into constructing something grand when socialite Lady Astor rolled up to the Sentinel, Yosemite Valley's only hotel, and deemed it "primitive."

Designed by Los Angeles architect Gilbert Stanley Underwood, The Ahwahnee is anything but unrefined, by design. Take the 24-foot-ceilings in the Great Lounge, with hand-painted beams and floor-to-ceiling windows that embellish the already showstopping view with their intricate stained-glass panels. Or the chandelier-lit dining room, where a gable-roofed ceiling reaches a 34-foot-tall peak and sugar pine roof trusses nod to the surrounding forests.

The Ahwahnee is almost an optical illusion. The scale of it is nothing less than ginormous when you're within its walls. But when you step outside, the lodge feels absolutely dinky compared to the monolithic granodiorite mountains surrounding it. It's no wonder its name—*ah-wah-nee*, a word of the indigenous Ahwahneechee, who lived here for centuries—means "land of the gaping mouth." Standing in Yosemite Valley, you can't help but to let your mouth fall open in awestruck wonder. Say it with me, "Aaaah."

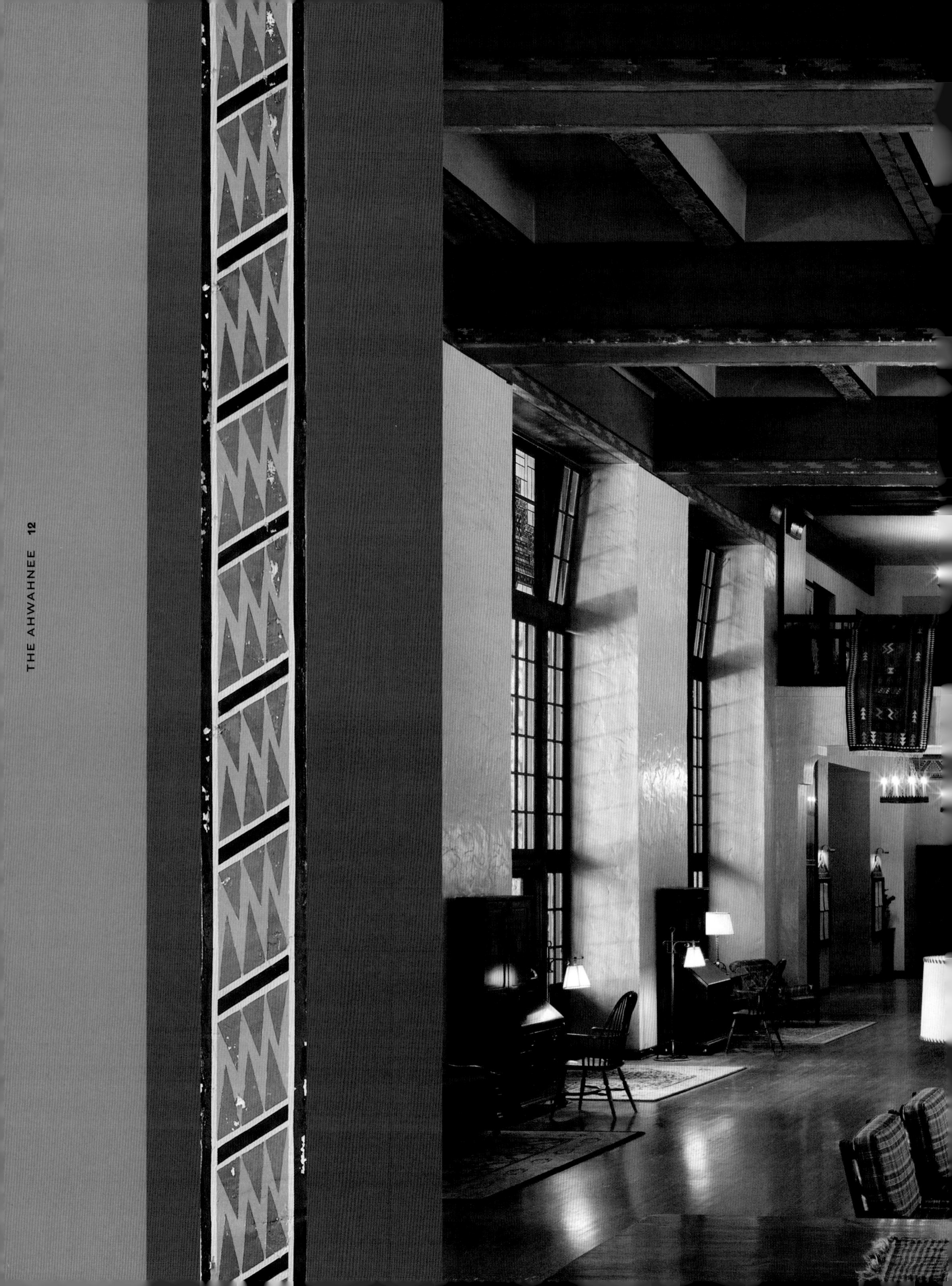

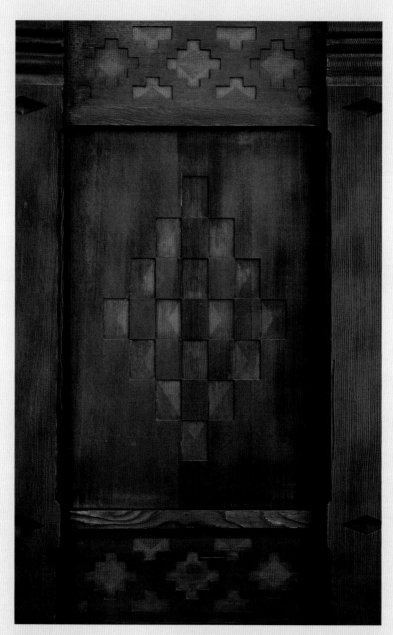

Nitty-gritty details abound inside The Ahwahnee, which opened in 1927. Just as in the wild forests outside, there are patterns everywhere you look— carved into the walls, ceilings, and floors.

This sitting area is an exercise in the power of symmetry and was tailor-made for playing board games and chitchatting the afternoon away. Artifacts and memorabilia are tucked behind the original wavy glass in the cabinets.

↑ Much of the lobby's furniture is original but has been reupholstered to stand up to generations of guests. While these fabric choices are contemporary, they wouldn't have been out of place a hundred years ago.

→ This is the best table in The Ahwahnee Dining Room (and reportedly where Queen Elizabeth II sat when she stayed here in 1983). Adding to the storybook appeal? The 34-foot-high exposed-beam ceiling, twinkling chandeliers, and the view over misty Yosemite Falls.

One of the cottages on the
grounds of The Ahwahnee.

Back in the day, California artist Robert Boardman Howard painted these linen-lined walls with Yosemite fauna, alongside a hand-hammered copper fireplace hood. It's in the Mural Room, which feels like you're in a time capsule. It's totally indulgent—not the type of room most of us normally get to sit around in, reading books and sipping hot cocoa.

↑ The chevron-paned, leaded-glass windows of the Library Suite can be flung open to peep out on Yosemite Falls, the highest in the park at 2,425 feet and taller than the Empire State Building.

→ Intricate motifs are even underfoot. Shown here: the sun-swept mosaics of the lobby floors.

Overleaf: A pianist plays classical and pop hits during the dinner rush, and totally hits the right note.

← The hand-painted beams of the Great Room are being restored. This space is an exercise in using multiple sources of light—ring chandeliers, table lamps, floor lamps—which lead your eye high and low, like a megawatt city skyline.

↑ "Granny chic" has come full circle, as evidenced by the draperies and four-post bed in the Library Suite. The teals and oranges in the color palette nod to the hues beyond the windows.

↑ Jeannette Dyer Spencer, who studied stained glass production at École du Louvre in Paris, designed the Great Room's stained-glass windows. Each one is different from the others, and watching the sun stream through them is aesthetic candy.

→ We visited The Ahwahnee in late winter before the trees began blooming again. But, honestly, the hotel's granite and concrete faux-wood exterior (a fire prevention measure) looks dynamite in all seasons.

The verticality of the main floor windows echoes the soaring monoliths of Yosemite Valley. They're so tall, they make even standard-size chairs and tables look like mini dollhouse furniture. The ochre-colored walls have a sheen that really bounces light around.

↑ Dark window and door muntins force your eyes outside.

→ No wonder Ansel Adams—born a city kid in San Francisco—was riveted by the majestic crest of Half Dome. It proudly greeted us on the way into The Ahwahnee, just as photo ready as ever.

← The year after the main lodge opened, the guest cottages were built in a Mission-meets-Arts & Crafts style so timeless that they could have been designed today.

↑ Another view of the Library Suite.

CRATER LAKE LODGE

Crater Lake National Park, Oregon

How small and insignificant can a person be made to feel? The stars at Crater Lake Lodge were like nothing I've ever seen. We visited during a new moon—when there is no glowing orb or sliver of light in sight—and it was so dark that we could see Andromeda, the galaxy beyond our galaxy. We were already standing in a national park, on the highest paved road in Oregon, overlooking the deepest lake in the country—and then to see something even more unforgettable like that. It's craziness.

The scene at this hideaway—which opened in 1915 and is perched on the rim of a volcanic caldera—is more of a home base for day hikers and lake peepers than a full-on resort. Practicality ruled when they were designing the place; it was constructed at the height of World War I, after all. With its unpeeled log beams and rubble stone masonry, it's meant to summon the feel of an Adirondack Great Camp. The structure spent decades down on its luck after the Great Depression, but, thankfully, nobody had the heart to knock it down. Subsequent interior renovations have installed or kept little charmers like squirrel andirons (a nod to the park's furry mischief-makers) and Stickley and Old Hickory furniture.

Really, when you're here, it's all about that lake. The water is 1,943 feet deep and preternaturally blue because it's fed only by snow and rain, with no murky rivers or creeks flowing into it. The lodge exterior feels old, but the lake itself is literally prehistoric; it was formed more than 7,700 years ago after Mount Mazama erupted and collapsed in on itself. And it's all right there in front you: the porch lined with rocking chairs drops straight down to the water's edge. In the distance, the peak of Wizard Island rises jauntily from the lake surface, as if to wink at you on the shore.

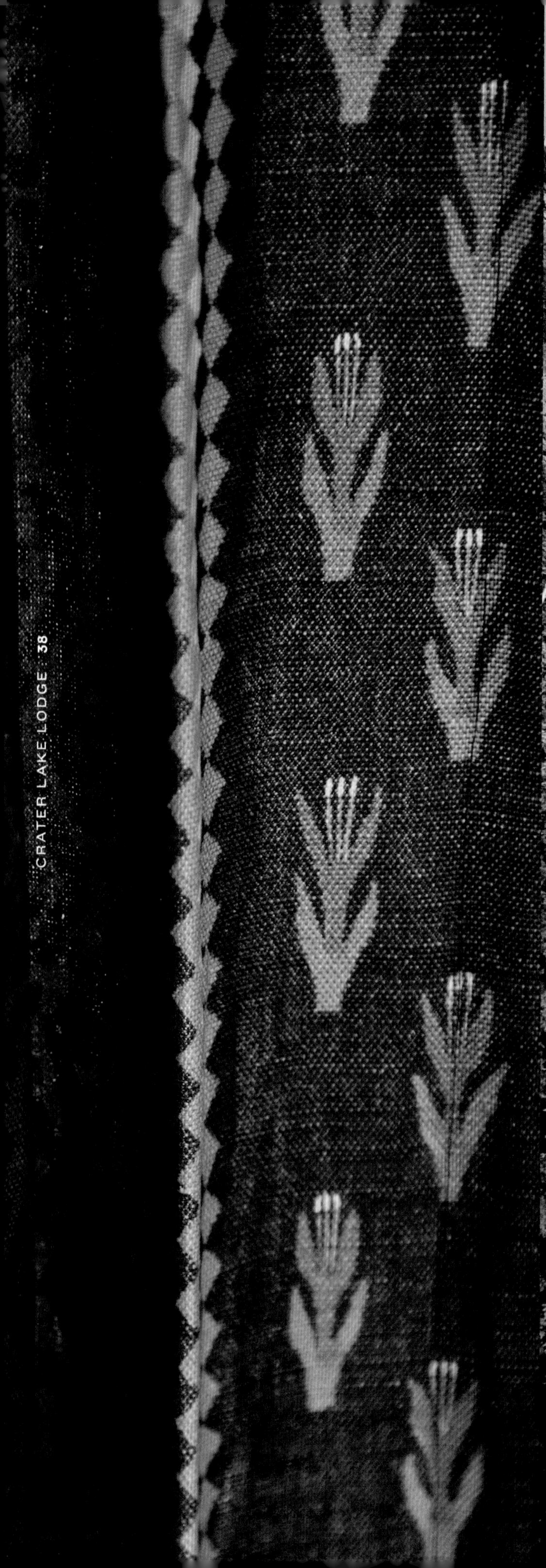

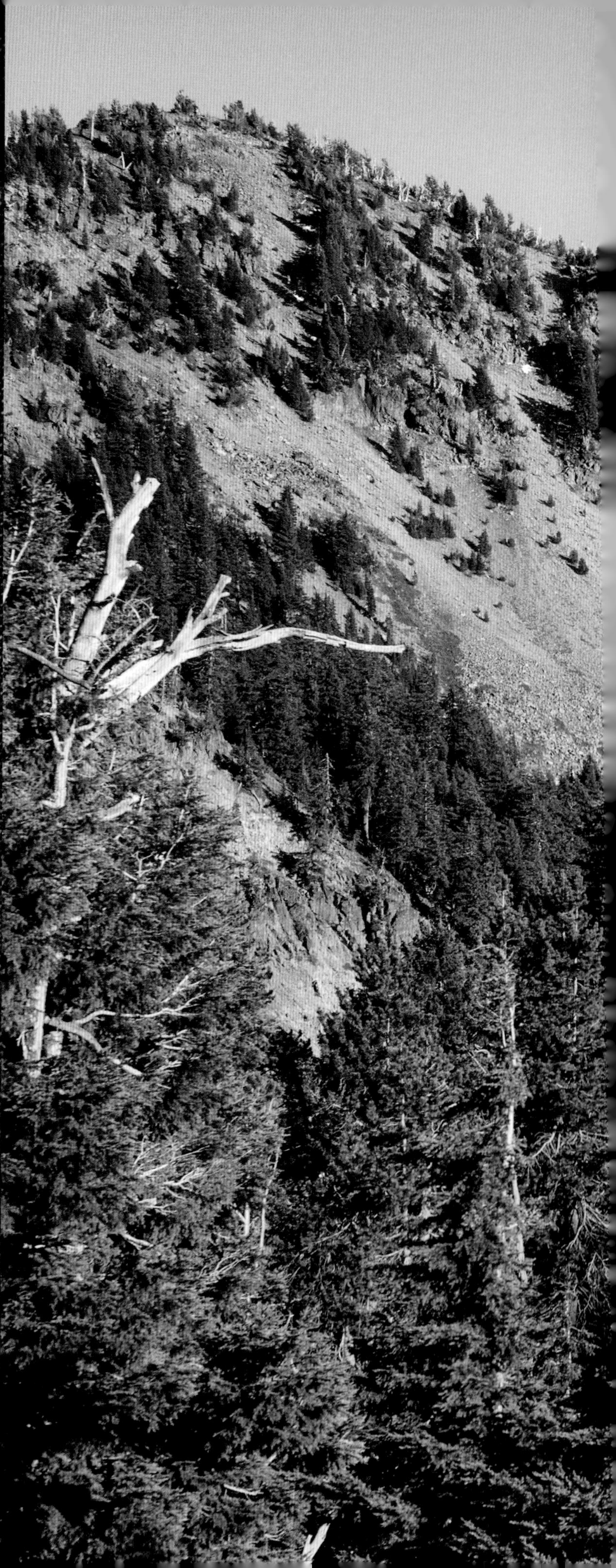

↑ The Crater Lake Lodge Dining Room has a panorama over the volcanic crater lake—one of the bluest on the planet, and the deepest in the United States at 1,943 feet.

→ In a recent revamp, architects sheathed inner areas with bark to up the woodsy factor. These wonderfully worn leather chairs are by Stickley Furniture, which has been making them pretty much the same way for eons.

The old stone fireplace in the lobby is the 1915 original—a good thing, because they don't often build them like they used to. The seating arrangement echoes the calming, symmetrical architecture.

Many of the guest rooms have their own plumply plush window seats—quintessential spots for perching, reading, and lake-peeping.

In this steep chalet roof, the dormers are like little eyes popping out.

→ Cut-stone steps hewn in the 1920s and '30s guide visitors on their lake-ogling quests.

↑ These cartoonish trees stand across the driveway from the lodge. We think windy days have something to do with their nearly nude wardrobe.

→ As you can see, designers went full throttle on the rustic thrills in the lobby, down to the forest-inspired coat racks.

Crater Lake's cutest long-term residents are arguably its golden-mantled ground squirrels, who feast on the area's native grasses and, as this guest room's lamp rendition shows, fallen nuts galore.

The lodge was reconstructed in the 1990s after falling headfirst into disrepair. Architects were able to salvage much of the original stonework, which they culled from nearby volcanic ledges and then reapplied as a veneer on a sturdy new cement foundation.

The tables on this side of the dining room have views of the lake. Dishes made with seasonal ingredients include marionberry cobbler, my favorite dessert from the lodge tour.

→ The fairly recent rehab of the lodge was done in such a respectful way that you can't tell if the materials are from the 1920s or today.

← We visited during a new moon, which is when the moon is not visible. As a result, the skies were so inky black that the Milky Way looked like this with the naked eye.

↑ Half the rooms face the sapphire-blue water, and those are where you want to stay.

CURRY VILLAGE

Yosemite National Park, California

Anyone who has ever been to Yosemite's Curry Village knows that it's not a Lodge with a capital L, like the rest of the retreats in this book. But that was by design. Tucked under Half Dome, it was founded as Camp Curry in 1899 by a couple of former teachers, David and Jennie Curry, who knew there needed to be an affordable alternative to fancy-pants hotels for explorers on a budget.

Curry Village advertised "a good bed and a clean napkin with every meal." Built on 48 acres of land formerly occupied by the Ahwahneechee tribe, among others, it was basically glamping. It once had a bowling alley, toboggan slide, and dance hall, and you could pay $12 and stay for a week, including meals. But when more and more lodging options appeared in the area, competition got fierce. To lure guests, David Curry devised an extravaganza of sorts—the Firefall—in which, after dark, he'd roar, "Let 'er go, Gallagher!" and have a literal bonfire pushed off Glacier Point far down to the rocky talus slope below—like a DIY firework. It's not an entertainment option they're offering these days; the Assistant Secretary of the Interior wisely told him to stop providing the spectacle in 1913. The ever-enterprising Currys made up for the financial loss quickly by putting in a swimming pool.

These days, what you'll find is all you need for a great family getaway—a series of canvas tents, hotel rooms, cabins, a pool, a mountaineering school, and beadboard-walled buildings with shuffleboard and oversized games (cue the Connect Four). I loved how haphazardly the wall paneling was installed, with some horizontal, some vertical, and even some at a diagonal. Even though these are some of the oldest buildings in Yosemite Valley, they look modern inside because they're all painted white. The napkins were clean too.

↑ Curry Village is very different from The Ahwahnee. It's got backpacker vibes, and there are board games and charm to spare.

→ This gathering space is in one of the oldest buildings in Yosemite Valley. It looks like they used different materials on every wall and ceiling, just slapping up what they had on hand without a game plan—which only adds to the patchwork, homey feel.

Made of unpeeled saplings,
the 20-foot-high Camp Curry
welcome sign was built in
1914 and reads "Welcome" on
your approach and "Farewell"
when you leave. It's so iconic,
it's included in the National
Register of Historic Places.

The interdenominational
Yosemite Valley Chapel was
built circa 1879 and designed in
Carpenter Gothic style.

↑ Your lodging options here include wood-floored canvas tent "cabins," standard rooms, and cabins like these—replete with baths, electricity, and wall heaters.

→ Don't forget your quarters. At Curry Village, you can phone home to talk about the day's exploits from a real pay phone.

The clean palette and simplicity
of materials is so modern.

Being at Curry Village is like being dropped off by your parents at summer camp. Only here, you'll find things like custom scenic bedspreads in lieu of your old bedroll.

EL TOVAR HOTEL

Whether you arrive by plane, train, or automobile—or in the saddle of a mule—the Grand Canyon will take your breath away. Part of it is that you're almost 7,000 feet above sea level and staring down at a more-than-six-million-year-old canyon that's bigger than all of Rhode Island. Built in 1905, El Tovar Hotel hugs the south rim and adds to the otherworldly experience. It's like a Swiss Chalet in the Alps but turned upside down.

We drove here from Las Vegas, and the juxtaposition of going from the Strip to the neon-less parade of hotels in Grand Canyon Village was a trip. But El Tovar Hotel itself is just what you'd imagine for a National Park lodge, with its dark wood beams, tucked-away mezzanine with a nightly piano player, and liberal displays of taxidermy. We stayed in the Mary Colter suite, named for the architect who designed a lot of the buildings in and around the Grand Canyon. Her rubble masonry Lookout Studio, inspired by ancient Puebloan homes, is an eight-minute walk from the lodge.

The star of El Tovar is undoubtedly the dining room, which is sheathed in local limestone and Oregon pine, with murals of the Hopi, Apache, Mojave, and Navajo. The view beyond the windows changes with the weather, from early morning mist to contrasting shadows in the harsh sunlight of high noon. During our stay, the service was really good; you're in a white-tablecloth restaurant, and it feels like it. We loved the regional menu that takes a lot of cues from the 1930s. You don't want to miss the El Tovar flapjacks at breakfast, which are skinnier than pancakes and better. They were transcendent, made of local blue cornmeal and served with honey pine nut butter and Arizona prickly pear syrup.

Even in our few nights at El Tovar, I felt the place had some level of curative, self-care properties. President Theodore Roosevelt vacationed here not once but twice shortly after he decamped the White House, as if to detox from one of the world's most thankless jobs. There's just something in the air here. These words, carved over the lodge entrance, really say it: "Dreams of mountains, as in their sleep they brood on things eternal."

Constructed just 20 feet from the Grand Canyon's edge, El Tovar Hotel opened in 1905. This entrance lobby was originally (and aptly) called the Rendezvous Room and has a chocolaty brown stained finish on the log-slab paneling and rafters.

The Grand Canyon Railway ferries visitors 64 miles in from Williams, Arizona, to the South Rim on restored classic trains, allowing a little more than three hours to explore the Grand Canyon. (The ride itself is a trip, with a Wild West shootout and the occasional cowboy train robbery.) El Tovar becomes much quieter when day-trippers decamp.

El Tovar Hotel was designed by Charles Whittlesey for the Atchison, Topeka and Santa Fe Railway and is a bit of a mishmash between a Swiss chalet and a Norwegian villa—with a shingled turret, mansard roofs, and tapered posts topped with trefoils.

↑ The Grand Canyon Railway trots out historic trains, like 1923 rail cars, to bring guests to its Grand Canyon Depot. Opened in 1910, this is the only primarily log-built depot that is still serving a working railroad.

→ The lobby mailbox is a throwback—and a reminder that before sending selfies, we sent postcards.

MEZZANINE LOUNGE
FOR EL TOVAR GUESTS

MAIL
PICKUP AT
9 A.M. MON. - FRI.

President Theodore Roosevelt proclaimed
the mile-deep Grand Canyon a national
monument in 1908 (it was made a National
Park in 1919). He wrote: "I want to ask you
to keep this great wonder of nature as it
now is . . . You cannot improve on it. The
ages have been at work on it, and man can
only mar it."

Generations have sat in the Old
Hickory rocking chairs lining
El Tovar's wraparound porches and
stared out at the iconic landscape.

Paintings of the canyon and area artifacts festoon the lobby.

All 78 rooms at El Tovar are different, but each one includes perks like bell service and air-conditioning. This is the Mary Colter Suite, named for the architect who did a lot of work in the region.

← When El Tovar Hotel was built—out of local limestone and Oregon pine—well-heeled guests called it the most elegant hotel west of the Mississippi.

↑ There are a lot of octagons within the architecture of El Tovar, including this view of the lobby from the upstairs mezzanine.

The dining room—with befitting Mission-style chandeliers and a fireplace on either side—has the best views of anywhere within the hotel. Try the braised lamb shank in pasilla sauce with corn and cotija polenta.

The lodge's next-door neighbor,
the Bright Angel Lodge
(designed by Mary Colter),
has an old-time soda fountain
through these painted doors.

The architects did a good job blending El Tovar into the landscape. It looks huge when you're inside but as miniature as mesquite bushes when you walk down the path and glance back at it.

GRAND CANYON NATIONAL PARK, ARIZONA **85**

As chief architect and decorator for the Fred Harvey Company, Mary Colter designed Hermit's Rest, Desert View Watchtower, and Lookout Studio, among other unmissable South Rim sights. This portrait hangs in the suite that bears her name.

Keep an eye out for the select
dates each year that the Grand
Canyon Railway runs their vintage
steam locomotives, including one
that dates to 1906.

LAKE MCDONALD LODGE

Glacier National Park, Montana

Sure, Europe beckoned. But in 1913, land speculator John Lewis felt he could bring the storybook style of Switzerland's alpine chalets back home to his rugged Montana. The Great Northern Railway was building an empire, a strand of jewels connected by train tracks. Lewis scooped up land alongside 472-foot-deep Lake McDonald and tasked Spokane firm Cutter and Malmgren with designing something "worthy of the park." No roads existed to the plot yet, so he had the building materials shipped in by boat and, come winter, skidded across the thick ice. It was worth it.

If I brought the family back to any of these, it would be Lake McDonald Lodge. It's the one I would live at. What can I say? I love a lake. Especially one where you can hop on a 1930s boat or rent a kayak and glide over the glass-clear water with snow-capped peaks reflected in the mirror. This one is so clear, it's almost disorienting; it has a photorealistic reflection. And coming into the lodge from the water is just how it was intended (they didn't build a road here until 1920, so the lakefront face is the true front of the hotel.) Try to get a waterfront room or, better yet, a cabin like we did, with mule deer for neighbors.

Despite its external beauty, the indoorsy stuff is even better. In the open, beamed lobby, hulking cedar logs rise three stories, ringed by balconies with stick-style railings. There's art everywhere, which isn't the case with every lodge. Paintings stud the walls alongside animalia from the region—elk, moose, mountain goats, and more, much of it part of Lewis's original collection.

You can walk right into the inglenook stone fireplace, which is so massive you don't sit around it, you sit inside it. In the concrete floors are Blackfoot, Cree, and Chippewa phrases that translate into "new life to those who drink here" and "looking toward the mountain."

The focal point of the entire lobby is the oversized rawhide parchment chandelier, which is a lone asymmetrical piece in the space. When we were there in May, it stayed light outside until 10 o'clock at night. To get the full effect of the chandelier, it's worth being patient for darkness to fall, when it truly brings the rustic razzle-dazzle.

Old Hickory chairs—made from inner-bark hickory shavings handwoven in a herringbone motif—have sat in the lobby of Lake McDonald Lodge for generations.

Stick-style railings and skyscraping
cedar columns lend a woodsy gravitas
to the lobby.

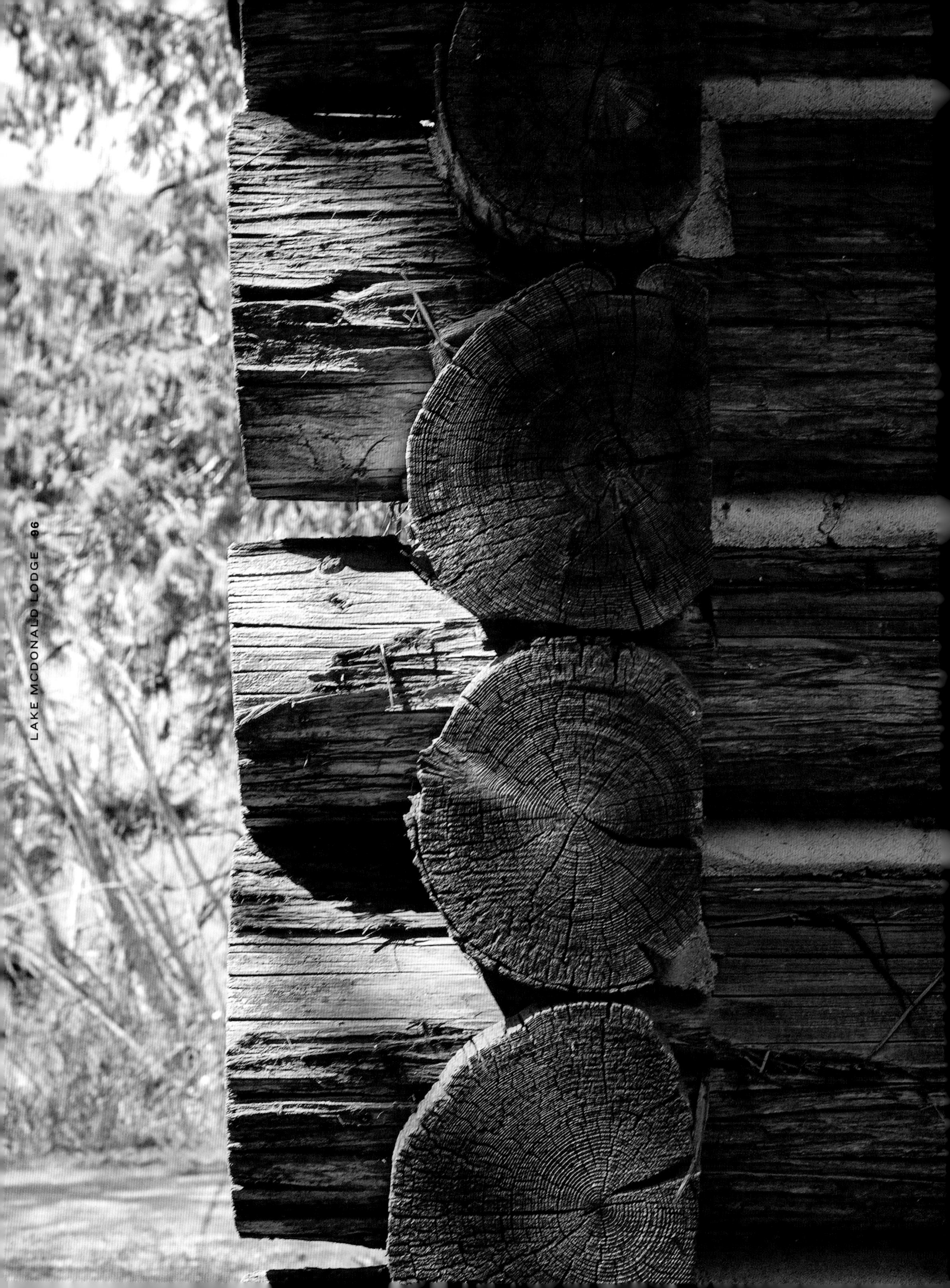

← Several guest cabins were built before the main lodge went up in 1913 and have the timeworn logs to prove it.

↑ Ironically, you'll want to BYO camera phone to take a photograph of this highly Instagrammable pay phone.

The comparatively low-ceilinged dining room predates the rest of the lodge and is sheathed in exposed logs.

Glacier's fleet of 17-seat red buses has been used since the 1930s to get visitors prime panoramas of the peaks. (The tops roll back for open-air views.) They're nicknamed "Jammers" because of the sound they used to make when drivers jammed them into gear on the steep curves.

← Keeping up on your correspondence is so much more delightful when you're perched at a lobby desk like this one, flanked by towering cedar logs.

↑ Lake McDonald Lodge fronts a pebbled beach. The lake was carved by glaciers way back in the Ice Age and is 472 feet deep.

The lobby's parchment chandelier was reportedly originally designed for The Prince of Wales Hotel in Alberta's Waterton Lakes National Park, with drawings by the area's indigenous Kainai tribe.

A communal dining table lined with Old Hickory chairs beckons in the lobby, where many of the taxidermy mounts were part of the original collection of lodge founder John Lewis.

Lake McDonald is famous for its
rainbow rocks, whose hues vary
from green to red depending on
how much iron is in them.

↑ Swiss chalets inspired the Lake
McDonald Lodge architecture,
but the use of regional materials
connect it to its Montana locale.

So much of this place's history is lost to time. But if lore is true, early Montana frontier artist Charlie Russell cut the petroglyphs into the lodge's concrete fireplace.

The stand-alone guest cabins that face the lake are ideal for families or shutterbugging bachelors.

→ At a camp store on the grounds of Lake McDonald Lodge we stocked up on provisions to make a quick PB&J and root beer picnic lunch.

← Some of the many trees surrounding Lake McDonald include western hemlock, paper birch, and lodgepole pine, which earned its moniker when it was used for (yes) lodge framework.

↑ The lobby's stucco-covered stone walls are now painted a warm hue that glows like a sunset.

Lake McDonald visitors can hop on an hour-long boat tour aboard the DeSmet, which has been whirling guests around the lake since 1930.

LAKE QUINAULT LODGE

Olympic National Park, Washington

Anyone who says all good things take time hasn't stayed at Lake Quinault Lodge. The cedar-shingled stunner was built in a zippy 53 days back in 1926, its construction crews working around the clock— even after dark, by the light of mammoth bonfires. They had to. Olympic National Park is in a literal rain forest, and they wanted to get it done in summer before the rainy season descended.

Slung along a lake, the place has the carefree feel of an East Coast summer camp, complete with a throwback indoor pool and lush shag carpet of lawn that rolls down to the lapping water. If a young Patrick Swayze and Jennifer Grey were to have the time of their lives anywhere, it would be here.

Encircled by towering Sitka spruce, Douglas fir, and western hemlocks, the V-shaped main lodge has a different vibe from the prototypical parkitecture. There are no boundless, soaring ceilings, no oversized rawhide chandeliers. But you don't miss them, thanks to other details that make it uniquely of its place—including a two-story rain gauge shaped like a totem pole that measures annual rainfall in feet, not inches. The hotshot architect behind its Northwest Regional design was starchitect Robert Reamer, who had designed Yellowstone's Old Faithful Inn more than two decades earlier.

The main lobby is warm and cozy, with an adjacent dining room, where you can eat in the same nook where President Franklin D. Roosevelt had lunch in 1937. When we were there, it felt like every single guest had dinner at that restaurant—young couples drinking wine; babies with their grandmas; Orange County soccer coaches; day hikers—before corralling around the lobby's crackling wood fires after dusk.

We bunked in a room in a nearby building, but it still faced the four-mile-long lake and its surrounding mist-shrouded mountains. Through the open screened windows, you can tell you're in a rain forest even in your sleep. As rain patters down on the trees, every drop of drizzle creates a white-noise machine sprung to life.

↑ A true-to-scale (well, presumably) Sasquatch greets guests in Lake Quinault Lodge, built in 1926 on the densely forested outskirts of Olympic National Park.

→ We got in a kayak to photograph the back of the lodge. It fronts 240-foot-deep Lake Quinault, where a wide, lush lawn rolls nearly to the water's edge.

The lobby furniture was recently refreshed and has a bit of a gentlemen's club aesthetic with its kelly greens and camel leather. It has the most interesting window treatments of any of the lobbies we visited, with tailored cornice boxes. Because there's so much wood in this room, bringing in some softness with fabric and a scalloped edge is a welcome touch.

← President Franklin D. Roosevelt was here in 1937—and if you're lucky, you can sit at the exact table where he lunched. He must have enjoyed his visit because nine months later he inked the bill that officially created Olympic National Park.

↑ If you're traveling with a crowd, consider booking The Boathouse. Built in 1923, it has eight bedrooms, a veranda, and The Beverly—the lodge's lone traditional suite. It takes up the entirety of the top floor and has sweeping 360-degree views.

↑ With apologies to international coffee chains, your morning jolt tastes better in a room like this.

→ This is an updated, sculptural version of a traditional Chesterfield sofa, upholstered in yummy green leather.

↑ An upper room in the main lodge, overlooking the lake.

→ Hydrangeas grow wild here. They're traditionally among the most painstaking members of the floral queendom to grow so are a particularly lovely sight. They typically bloom here August through October.

Ferns and moss thrive in the deliciously damp Olympic Peninsula, which has the same diversity of plant species as the British Isles. Endearing details abound, from the diamond cutouts in the shutters to the fish motif on the shed.

The rain gauge at Lake Quinault Lodge was designed to measure precipitation in feet, not inches—which makes sense in a place known for getting a whopping 12 feet of rain per year (next to Seattle's comparatively skimpy 37 inches).

COASTAL CALIFORNIA
REDWOODS PLANTED 1930

← Proof that "just add water" works? Some of the largest trees in the nation are in the rain forests of the Olympic Peninsula. Just a short walk from the lodge, you'll see the largest western red cedar on earth. It's 174 feet tall, with a 63.5-foot circumference.

↑ In the evening, every seat around the fireplace of the main lobby was filled. The room truly had a communal atmosphere, with strangers chitchatting into the wee hours.

↑ Large-scale and small-scale patterns mix beautifully here, especially with the notes of raspberry, cream, and deep collegiate-green in the color palette.

→ The main entrance has incredible symmetry. You look right through the lobby to the back deck and on down to the lake.

A time lapse of photos shows
the lodge, which was designed
by Seattle architect Robert
Reamer, being built in a mere
53 days.

Old Glory is particularly glorious when it's hung adjacent to timeworn cedar shingles.

Indoor pools aren't something
you commonly see in a woodsy
lodge. This one suits the locale,
in wood and stone, and is heated
seven days a week year-round.

3FT 3IN

4^{FT} 0^{IN} ⊗

7^{FT} 3^{IN} ⊗

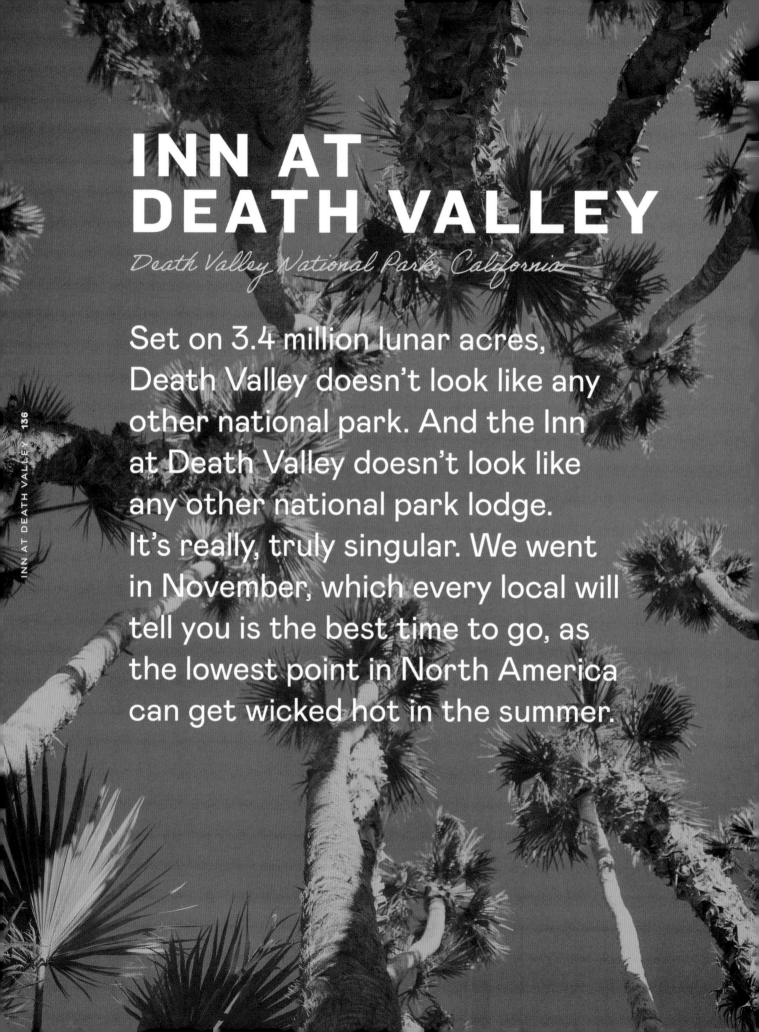

INN AT
DEATH VALLEY

Death Valley National Park, California

Set on 3.4 million lunar acres, Death Valley doesn't look like any other national park. And the Inn at Death Valley doesn't look like any other national park lodge. It's really, truly singular. We went in November, which every local will tell you is the best time to go, as the lowest point in North America can get wicked hot in the summer.

To get here, we flew to Las Vegas, hopped into our rental car, and drove an hour and 45 minutes through Mars. After a quick detour at Zabriskie Point—where the sediments from a 5-million-year-old lake are so cinematic they made a movie here in 1970—we saw the Oasis (which includes the Inn at Death Valley). It is so aptly named, it's bananas. Having driven past the rippling salt hills and sights like Badwater Basin and Dante's View, it loomed like a mirage—a sprawling, Mission-style resort dotted with date palm trees, carpets of green grass, and fragrant bougainvillea that rises seemingly out of nowhere, thanks to ancient subterranean aquifers.

The Pacific Coast Borax Company had been shipping the antiseptic mineral (commonly used as a cleaner) out of Death Valley since 1881 and opened the original inn in 1927 to pad their income. Nearly instantly, it became an escape for Old Hollywood stars. Clark Gable was here. Marlon Brando too. And why not? The spring-fed pool covered in mosaic tiles to mirror the surrounding palm fronds is 87 degrees. Tennis greens and the lowest golf course in the world await on the magical grounds designed by star landscape architect Daniel Hull, who was responsible for planning the landscape in many of the national parks. Indoors, the building and interiors were conceived by Albert C. Martin Sr, who helped design Los Angeles City Hall and the Million Dollar Theater, a 1918 movie palace. The architecture feels very Spanish Colonial revival, with arched windows, ironwork chandeliers, and cinnamon-hued exposed beams studding the ceilings. The color palette was taken directly from the surrounding badlands. With its reddish-orange roof tiles and stone or stucco walls, it feels like a Hollywood movie-set version of an original California Spanish mission.

Recently revamped to the tune of $100 million, the Inn at Death Valley feels very upscale—like a Vacation with a capital V. It may be the only national park lodge where you can hike or sightsee in the morning and sip a frothy daiquiri poolside in the afternoon.

My advice: book a casita, and they'll loan you a golf cart for zooming around the premises. And prepare to fully unplug and relax, especially as the sun sets behind the purple mountains.

The artfully eroded landscape of Zabriskie Point was created when Furnace Creek Lake dissipated some 5 million years ago.

Originally known as Furnace Creek Inn, the lodge opened in 1927 with just 12 rooms. It was upgraded and expanded over the years to look like a Mission-style citadel.

↑ The age-old mystique of California's Spanish Missions inspired the hotel's architecture. Its color palette takes its cues from the badlands of Zabriskie Point and Artists Drive.

→ With its resort-like feel and proximity to La La Land, this was a Hollywood hangout (former guests include Marlon Brando, Carole Lombard, and Clark Gable).

Overleaf: The palm tree–flanked pool is spring-fed and stays a cozy 87 degrees.

← Arches are used throughout the Inn at Death Valley, framing palatial views. The house-made date bread at breakfast on the patio is not to be missed; you'll want to bring it home with you.

↑ The Oasis at Death Valley is a resort that contains both the Inn at Death Valley and the Ranch at Death Valley. The name Oasis really is appropriate, because when you get here, you've essentially driven through Mars and landed smack-dab on an island of green.

Overleaf: The lobby feels luxurious, with its rich, jewel-toned fabrics and barley-twist table legs. Above it all, open beams supply a storied feel. This room wouldn't have the same effect without them.

← It's worth stopping in at the Inn's sister property, Ranch at Death Valley, to belly up to the bar. Called The Last Kind Words Saloon, it was built on the site of a former working ranch and features veritable herds of taxidermy and antique "wanted" posters for Wild West outlaws.

↑ Just off the lobby of the Inn, the library has books you can check out and carved wooden desks if you need to sneak in some WFL (work from lodge) emails.

↑ Recently revamped, 22 private casitas are just a golf cart ride away on the lush, green property.

→ Tiered fountains on the dining patio gurgle, adding to a Mediterranean feel.

↑ Most guest rooms have views of the Oasis Garden or Panamint Mountains beyond.

→ Ask for the stone-clad suite overlooking the spring-fed swimming pool.

A natural spring snakes around the bougainvillea-shrouded property.

These towering California fan palms are native to Baja and the Sonoran Desert, but they thrived here when they were introduced. They can grow up to 60 feet tall, with six-foot-long crowns of "fan" leaves. The two top tables in the lobby overlook the main entrance (and golf cart parking) below, and the mountains beyond.

OLD FAITHFUL INN

Yellowstone National Park, Wyoming

When you drive into Yellowstone, the welcoming committee are bison. Hundreds and hundreds of them, scruffy and thrilling—and right there alongside (or even in) the road. As we drove in for this photo shoot in late May, snowflakes swirled around us. They were the biggest, most "movie" version of snowflakes I've ever seen. It was all a fittingly untamed prelude to the tallest log structure on earth, Old Faithful Inn.

Built to edge the famous 140-foot-high geyser for which it's named, Old Faithful Inn is hard to beat. The 1904 lodge was designed by then-29-year-old architectural wunderkind Robert Reamer. Apparently, he made it a little asymmetrical and wonky on purpose to reflect the inevitable chaos of nature. Unlike the style of other, more buttoned-up lodges, some of Old Faithful's architectural choices look like they were designed on the fly—e.g., things don't line up; windows are placed in a cockamamie scheme. We liked sitting back in the lobby's hickory sapling chairs (most of them 1904 originals) and gawking. It's all structurally sound, of course, but it doesn't quite look like it.

Wandering through, you'll see staircases that look like they were designed around the knuckled knots of fallen junipers and a dining room that's preserved to perfection. We stayed in the old part of the lodge, where the rooms have wood-paneled walls and ceilings. There is no drywall in there! The rooms are as charming as you can get in a national park lodge, and they clank, with their claw-foot tubs and old heating systems. It's all bubbles and steam, inside and out.

In the lobby itself, the four-sided fireplace rising to the rafters was built from 500 tons of rhyolite, made by ancient volcanic eruptions here and culled from the nearby Black Sand Basin. Reamer knew just what he was doing—it really is wild. If you peer 72 1/2 feet up, you'll see the Crow's Nest, a de facto indoor tree house inspired by Reamer's own childhood fantasy. In the lodge's early days, a string quartet would climb to it after dinner and play as guests danced across the gleaming lobby floors below. Sitting in the mezzanine now, it feels like you have a front-row seat for going back in time.

↑ This land is their land: Bison have lived in Yellowstone since the prehistoric era. Bulls can top out at 2,000 pounds—as much as a rhino. In other words, don't get close to the buffalo! (This image was taken with a really long lens.)

→ As if to attempt the same loftiness as its namesake, Old Faithful Inn's exposed log frame is seven stories high—nearly a skyscraper by 1904 standards.

Overleaf: The geyser erupts about 20 times a day with a steam temperature of 350 degrees.

The original part of the inn is called the Old House and retains its peeled-log walls. These rooms cost four dollars a night when it opened.

A raised wooden boardwalk leads around the Upper Geyser Basin, where there are some 150 geothermal features near the cheekily named Firehole River.

Amenities in the Old House
guest rooms often include built-
in window seats, plus cute little
in-room sinks.

Log-framed gables on the roof (some of them intentionally supported by gnarled wood) and shingles that are a yard long add to the inn's folktale effect.

The lodge was wired for electricity when it opened in 1904, but since the technology was still rare, the inn's 29-year-old architect, Robert Reamer, chose candlestick-like fixtures for lighting. The knobby, gnarled wooden brackets aren't structurally necessary; Reamer included them solely for their wow factor.

Bison forage for leafy greens nine to eleven hours a day. On our drive into the park, they started appearing before us one by one, and then there were hundreds.

Times posted inside the lobby list Old Faithful's expected geyser eruptions. Everyone wanders outside and waits and watches. Yellowstone predicts when 6 of its 500 geysers will spew next at nps.gov.

The inn's windows are arranged so haphazardly they almost look like constellations when light pours in.

↑ After nightfall, the intentional
asymmetry of the lodge becomes
even more apparent.

→ Exposed log scissor trusses ornament the ceiling
of the dining room. Old Hickory designed the Old
Faithful Inn dining chairs and shipped hundreds of
them here in 1904. Architect Reamer considered
them the finishing touches, and he was right; they're
still being used more than 115 years later.

When we visited, the snow came out of nowhere, and we couldn't help but run outside to get a glimpse. The snowflakes that day were cartoonishly large and sticky. Cue some impromptu snowball fights.

Many of the bedrooms in the Old House have claw-foot tubs and no showers. When you walk around outside in the snow looking at geyser pools that are a zillion degrees, it's wonderful to come back to your room and soak in a piping hot tub.

← Heat from the inn's in-room radiators can help dry your gear off if you get into snowball free-for-alls.

↑ There are hiking trails from the inn to further geysers, Mallard Lake, 200-foot-tall Fairy Falls, and more. Just beware of Yellowstone's grizzly and black bears.

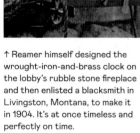

↑ Reamer himself designed the wrought-iron-and-brass clock on the lobby's rubble stone fireplace and then enlisted a blacksmith in Livingston, Montana, to make it in 1904. It's at once timeless and perfectly on time.

In the early 20th century, the Crow's Nest landing—built under the tippy top part of the gable roof—acted as a stage of sorts for the string quartets that played after supper.

PARADISE INN

Mount Rainier National Park, Washington

Decades before local and salvaged became buzzwords, the architects behind this fairytale chalet—built in 1916 in the shadow of Mount Rainier on the former hunting grounds of the Yakama and Puyallup peoples, among others—used yellow cedar trees that had died in a nearby wildfire to create the lodge's open timber frame. The result looks like the greatest Lincoln Log set ever made.

Inside Paradise Inn, the exposed beams are echoed by much of the furniture, which was handmade by German expat carpenter Hans Fraehnke. Starting in 1916, he arrived seven springs in a row (reportedly in wire-framed glasses and sporting a walrus mustache). He had to hike through drifts of March snow to reach the inn and built everything from the 14-foot-long, cedar-slab tables to the four Alaskan cedar throne chairs. Fraehnke intentionally built the latter to be 6 feet tall so that anyone who sits in them feels teensy and tucked away compared to the vast panorama beyond the windows.

When we stayed at Paradise Inn to photograph it in September, we experienced all four seasons within a couple of hours, including rain that poured sideways and a dusting of sugary snow. It was stunning! But there was a problem: Mount Rainier, a 14,411-foot active volcano, had gone into hiding for days—days!—under a thick quilt of clouds. Because of the crappy weather, the lobby was bustling with day hikers and backpackers sitting in the glow of the big stone fireplaces, snacking on M&M's, and playing Scrabble.

I loved taking in the vaulted ceiling, which was grand and overwhelming in a good way, and the intricate details everywhere, including hand-painted columns and lanterns adorned with local flora, like Cascade mountain-ash—beloved by grosbeak birds for its sweet berries. We sat overlooking it all in the wraparound mezzanine when, one by one, the people below began darting through the French doors to the outside. For ten minutes, the sun was out, and the peak of Mount Rainier emerged—proud and perfect in its much-deserved spotlight.

← In between rain and snowstorms, folks camped out in the lobby for wholesome extracurriculars like board games and dominoes while waiting for the weather to pass.

↑ Mount Rainier is so whopping that it creates its own weather patterns. We spent our first few days here waiting for this moment when the clouds peeled back and revealed the 14,411-foot peak.

↑ The guest rooms in the 1916 part of the 121-room lodge have built-in desks tucked within the dormer windows. They feel a little like boarding school dormitory bedrooms in Switzerland.

→ This color palette—a sophisticated grassy green against mauve drapes—isn't easy to pull off. If anyone knows what exact paint color this green is, please send the author a message.

↑ In autumn, the leaves of the
mountain-ash turn nearly as
scarlet as its berries. These
are so photogenic (and all over
the place, here) that they were
hand-painted on the lobby
lanterns.

→ Almost no surface evaded the
paintbrush. In the dining room,
everything from the columns to
the table details to the wainscot
(a confident eggplant hue) got a
layer of color. Above it all, another
painting of Mount Rainier provides
a view under the eaves.

The upper mezzanine wraps all the way around the lobby, and little private lounge areas are tucked between the beams. It was the best place to hang out because you could see out the dormer windows to get an instant read on the weather and note if the clouds were lifting—then go back to your checkers.

On a mountain like this, it can go from rain to sun to rain to snow again in mere moments.

MOUNT RAINIER NATIONAL PARK, WASHINGTON

← You don't have to get into your car to go hiking here; you can just start walking. There are 240 miles of trails in Mount Rainier, many leaving right outside your door to see the rushing waters of 72-foot-tall Myrtle Falls, or the glaciers along the 6-mile Skyline Trail.

↑ It's sort of meta, looking at a photo of the lodge itself from right inside your room. This was one of the quietest lodges we stayed in for this book, ensconced in our log beds.

Beams hewn of Alaska cedar
create a lot of the structural
framework. Dressed up with
hand-painted Swiss floral
motifs, the posts in the dining
room have the effect of an
enchanted forest.

Leaf peepers who flock to New England might want to re-route. Between late September and mid-October, Mount Rainier looks like it was painted by number—with garnet red huckleberries and larch dotting the landscape.

Inspired by the woodwork of the
Bavarian alps, the piano has been
here since the lodge opened its
doors. (President Harry Truman
tickled these ivories during his
1945 visit.) There is often a pianist
stationed here, thumbing through
the 1920s sheet music hidden in the
bench and jamming out old standards.

The lodge's porters wheel in wood every hour to keep the home fires burning.

↑ During a 1930s remodel, the original Japanese lanterns were replaced with parchment ones, each lovingly hand-painted to depict flora of the mountain.

ZION LODGE

Zion National Park, Utah

We call it the "Canyon Hug."
There is something about being in
the middle of a gorge that's been
inhabited by humans for 8,000
years, surrounded by 200-million-
year-old sandstone rocks, that
is the coziest thing ever. Adding
to the snug mood of Zion Lodge
itself is the fact that it has almost
a collegiate atmosphere: it's made
up of several buildings set by the
Virgin River and fronting a big,
central lawn that's a lot like a
campus quad.

Built in 1925, using lumber toted down from the mesa by draw and pulley, the lodge is a lesson in fortitude. Flattened by a fire in the sixties, it was rebuilt anew in just 100 days. Be sure to book one of the 40 cabins, which are original, designed by Ahwahnee architect Gilbert Stanley Underwood in the 1920s. They're not quite as enterprising as the nests that Zion's California condors build into the surrounding cliffs, but they're superb: exposed exterior framing, open-beam ceilings, and Navajo Sandstone chimneys—the works.

The lobby is modest, especially by traditional lodge standards. But that lush, grassy lawn makes up for it—with people splayed out in little groups soaking in the sun. And it's all centered around an ancient Fremont cottonwood that dapples shade over the throngs like *The Giving Tree*. We love that you can only drive to the lodge if you're staying there; otherwise, you have to take a shuttle. It keeps traffic and tourists to a minimum. And when the day's last shuttle departs the canyon at 6 p.m. and dusk falls over this cathedral of sandstone, it is like opting to stay on campus during the summer when all the other students have left. It's just you and Zion, the wild turkeys, and the gray foxes, living your best lives.

A Fremont cottonwood tree shades the carpet of grass fronting Zion Lodge, originally built in 1924 at the canyon floor. In the background, you can see the solar-powered shuttle buses that drop off the day visitors who use the lodge as base camp for their hikes.

← The main lodge was rebuilt in the 1990s after a fire flattened the original in 1966.

↑ Zion Canyon was carved over millions of years by the waters of the Virgin River.

↑ This looks like it was
photographed by drone, but
it wasn't. On hikes here, you
can get the same bird's-eye
view as Zion's own California
condors—famous for their
10-foot wingspans.

→ Original, single-suite cabins
with screen doors line the
campus and are so enchanting.

An interior of one of the guest cabins. You'll know when your neighbor has been on a hike through the Narrows—which leads 15 miles through a slot canyon of the Virgin River—when they leave their wet gear draped over their cabin's balcony railing.

When the native Fremont cottonwood trees find themselves rooted where they can slurp up plenty of water, they can grow 10 to 20 feet a year.

The little remote-controlled
fireplaces in the guest cabins
are ideal for upping the snug
factor on a cool night.

↑ A footbridge over the Virgin River brings guests to the Angels Landing trailhead.

Overleaf: This cluster of guest cabins was designed to blend in beautifully with their surroundings.

See Zion on the back of a trusty steed. Horseback rides are available to the Court of Patriarchs (sandstone cliffs), around the four-mile Sand Bench Trail loop and more.

Old Hickory rocking chairs await on the porch outside the main lodge.

Since cars aren't allowed unless
you're staying at the lodge,
the roads are mostly used by
bicyclists and Zion's mule deer.
Visit in May or June and you
may see one of their spotted
fawns.

A detail of one guest cabin's
custom bed frames.

← The menu at the lodge's Red Rock Grill features a lot of local ingredients, like Arizona prickly pear in vinaigrette and Utah apple cider on grilled pork chops.

↑ We found zilch Wi-Fi and cell service at Zion, which made it a truly unplugged escape.

↑ Gray foxes dart the manicured grounds after dusk.

→ Zion was recently certified as an International Dark Sky Park. Translation: the man-made lights in the area are kept as low as possible after nightfall so the stargazing is "extra."

The authors would like to thank:
René Mack, Betsy O'Rourke, Rick Hoeninghausen,
Hinch Knece, Andy Stiles, Marc Duchame, Gerard
Steffan, Sam Langner, Lisa Cesaro, Robin Garrison,
Daniel Rodriguez, and Joe DePlasco.

Special shout-out to:
Miles, Reid, Frida, Florence, and Guy.

THE AUTHORS

Rob Schanz is a San Francisco–based photographer. He has the unique ability to make the viewers of his images feel as if they are in the moment with him, often finding beauty in some of the simplest things.

ROBSCHANZ.COM

David Tsay is an advertising and branding photographer. He resides in Los Angeles with his husband, Jesse, and their chaotic Golden Retriever, Gus.

DAVIDTSAY.COM

Kathryn O'Shea-Evans is a Colorado-based writer and author with bylines in the *New York Times* and the *Wall Street Journal*. She spent a couple of her undergraduate college summers working in National Park lodges and is as indoorsy as it gets.

KATHRYNOSHEAEVANS.COM

Max Humphrey is a Portland, Oregon-based interior designer. After working in TV and film production and touring the U.S. and England as the bass player in a punk rock band signed to a major record label, he discovered a passion for interior design. His trademark lived-in, layered look has earned him accolades, including being named a "Next Wave" designer by *House Beautiful* and one of *Country Living's* 100 most creative people. His first coffee table book, *Modern Americana*, was released in 2021.

MAXHUMPHREY.COM

First Edition
27 26 25 24 23   5 4

**Text © 2023 by Max Humphrey
and Kathryn O'Shea-Evans**

PHOTOGRAPHIC CREDITS:

David Tsay © 2023: cover, 4, 10–11, 15, 17, 19, 20, 21–25, 27–31, 32TR, 32BL, 32BR, 35, 36–55, 56, 60–61, 68, 70, 72–75, 77–82, 84–86, 88BL, 88BR, 94–96, 98, 100, 101, 103, 105, 106, 108, 109, 136, 138–155, 159, 164, 169, 171, 177, 202–204, 208, 210, 212–213, 215, 217, 218, 220, 221, 224

Rob Schanz © 2023: 10, 14, 16, 18, 26, 32TL, 33 all, 34, 58–59, 62–67, 71, 76, 83, 87, 88T, 89T, 89B, 90, 92–93, 97, 99, 102, 104, 107, 110, 111, 112, 114–135, 156, 158, 160–163, 165–168, 170, 172–175, 176 all, 180–199, 200, 205–207, 209, 211, 214, 216, 219

Courtesy Max Humphrey: 9

Published by Gibbs Smith
P.O. Box 667 Layton, Utah 84041
1.800.835.4993 orders
gibbs-smith.com

Designed by Part and Parcel
partandparcel.la

Printed and bound in China

Gibbs Smith books are printed on either recycled, 100% post-consumer waste, FSC-certified papers or on paper produced from sustainable PEFC-certified forest/controlled wood source. Learn more at pefc.org.

Library of Congress
Control Number: 2022940156
ISBN: 978-1-4236-6134-4